CU00860004

THE BEST BEDTIME STORIES FOR CHILDREN

The Ultimate Collection of Short Mindful Tales for a Relaxing Night-Time Routine for You and Your Child

Rosa Knight

© Copyright 2021 - All rights reserved.

The content contained within this book may not be reproduced, duplicated or transmitted without direct written permission from the author or the publisher.

Under no circumstances will any blame or legal responsibility be held against the publisher, or author, for any damages, reparation, or monetary loss due to the information contained within this book. Either directly or indirectly.

Legal Notice

This book is copyright protected. This book is only for personal use. You cannot amend, distribute, sell, use, quote or paraphrase any part, or the content within this book, without the consent of the author or publisher.

Disclaimer Notice

Please note the information contained within this document is for educational and entertainment purposes only. All effort has been executed to present accurate, up to date, and reliable, complete information. No warranties of any kind are declared or implied. Readers acknowledge that the author is not engaging in the rendering of legal, financial, medical or professional advice. The content within this book has been derived from various sources. Please consult a licensed professional before attempting any techniques outlined in this book.

By reading this document, the reader agrees that under no circumstances is the author responsible for any losses, direct or indirect, which are incurred as a result of the use of information contained within this document, including, but not limited to, — errors, omissions, or inaccuracies.

Table of Contents

Introduction

Reading bedtime stories yields numerous benefits for parents and children the same. The fixed daily practice of a bedtime story before resting can improve the child's mental health, language authority, and coherent reasoning skills. The storyteller-audience relationship makes an emotional bond between the parent and the child. Due to "the quality of the imitative intuition" of a child, the parent and the stories that they tell go about as a model for the child to follow.

Bedtime stories are additionally helpful for training the child conceptual excellencies, for example, compassion, benevolence, and discretion, as most children are said to be "normally thoughtful when they have encountered or can envision the feelings of others". Thus, bedtime stories can be utilized to examine darker subjects, for example, passing and racism. As the bedtime stories expand in the topic, the child "will widen in their origination of the lives and feelings of others".

It is never too soon to acquaint your baby with the universe of stories. Specialists recommend that you begin reading them baby stories from an early age to help her imagination. You can do the reading so anyone might hear a habit while you're as yet pregnant, as children perceive their mom's voice in the belly.

Putting time aside to peruse stories consistently is a good habit. Bedtime and naptime are the best times. Making reading a piece of nighttime routine would enable your baby to quiet down and comprehend that it's time to rest. Set the time somewhere close to 6.30 pm and 8.30 pm. whenever after that can make your little one tired.

Bedtime stories are an extraordinary method to improve communication among you and your baby. She will cherish gazing at the brilliant pictures and have specific good time tuning in to the fantasies. Here are various benefits:

1. Creates correspondence:

Story reading helps in the development of children, oral relational abilities, listening capacities, memory, and language acknowledgment skills. It is an excellent method to reinforce her jargon and different sentence structures from an early age.

With time and age, your baby will figure out how to discuss through non-verbal communication, verbal strategies, tuning in, and composed words simply like you.

Children would have heard all the sounds required to communicate in their local language when they turn one. The more you read, the more the child is presented to words.

2. Social and emotional development:

Outlines and stories go connected at the hip, and your baby can create thoughts regarding different toys, creatures, flying creatures, etc. You will discover her utilization of new words to think, feel, and express her feelings.

3. Psychological skills:

Sometime before your baby has begun talking, she is gripping data about the language by tuning in to the stories you read. This will surely receive rewards when your child begins her training.

Children around ten months can figure out how to turn pages and tune in to new words. As your little one keeps on developing, she would take in the specialty of reading from left to right. Infants, who are around a year old, can build up their critical thinking skills by tuning in to bedtime stories.

4. Improves consideration:

Connecting with your baby in bedtime stories is a fantastic method to assist her with getting settled with the reading habit. It is, in fact, a beneficial and sound habit. You can improve her consideration skills by reading to her consistently.

5. Mitigates nervousness:

It is an excellent approach to loosen up her mind and body before hitting the hay. Even if he/she is overstimulated, story reading will assist her with engaging in a completely different world and alleviate from all the tensions.

6. Improves character and information:

As your baby develops, she may fire searching up for specific individuals and draw motivation from them. Reading time is the ideal time to impact the little one and show them life exercises. This can improve her character and information.

7. Turns into a habit:

At the point when you make story-reading your little one's everyday practice, it turns into a habit and a piece of her life. Step by step, reading turns into joy, and you don't need to request that she read after she grows up. Further down the road, the reading may make way for composing.

Tips for Parents:

Try not to make a story reading repetitive to your baby and yourself. Keep it so intriguing that she anticipates this sort of holding with you consistently.

1. Using different feelings and expressive sounds while reading the story encourages the social and emotional development of your baby.

2. As you read, make your child check and answer inquiries to advance social development and thinking skills.

3. Let her mimic sounds, perceive pictures, and learn words.

4. Readout with energy, happiness, and closeness. It encourages them to get related to books.

5. Cuddling while at the same time, reading causes your baby to feel associated, safe, and warm.

6. Sing rhymes and make amusing creature sounds.

7. Don't stress over reading a similar story over and over. Infants cherish and gain from reiteration.

8. Turn off interruptions like TV or radio.

9. By overstating the 'oo' sound in the moon and utilizing words like quiet, you can invigorate associations in the piece of your baby's cerebrum that handles language sounds. The part is known as the sound-related cortex.

10. Remember that the association with your baby is the key to making the most uptime story-reading.

How Stories Feed Imaginations

Each child is brought into the world with imagination, allowing them the chance to envision something that they haven't encountered. A sound imagination is the place inventiveness starts, empowering children to develop into innovative grown-ups. For the children in danger, we serve, inventiveness and critical thinking are essential skills they will require long into their future.

Innovative play is related to expanded inventive execution years after the fact, which implies solid imaginations get ready children for increasingly effective and gainful lives. Being an imaginative grown-up doesn't really mean turning into a painter or stone carver either; genuinely, any creative speculation starts with the capacity to envision another reality. This is the reason we are so dedicated to opening up the imaginations and innovativeness of the children we serve. Supporting them in learning how to envision another reality for themselves is perhaps the best thing we can accomplish for them.

How Healthy Imaginations Make Children More Resilient

Children with progressively created imaginations have a more remarkable capacity to manage pressure and exceptional feelings. Rather than in a split second feeling overpowered, they figure out how to ace their feelings utilizing their imaginations. If a child fears beasts, he can make up a story about chasing down the creature and startling it to transform it into something different. This capacity to self-manage benefits children when they become grown-ups by method for diminished hostility and the ability to endure postponed gratification.

Significance of reestablishing rest

Reading storybooks over and over enables preschool children to learn words. What's more, dozing soon after learning something extra encourages memory combination and helps to learn in more established children and grown-ups. The present examination investigated how rest advances word learning in preschool children utilizing a common storybook reading task. Children either read a similar story or different stories and either rested after the stories or remained awake. Children's word maintenance was tried 2.5 h later, 24 h later, and after seven days. Results exhibit substantial, diligent impacts for both rehashed readings and rest union on small kids' word learning.

Put them to sleep when they are drained.

Parents ought to be careful about playing dynamic games before bedtime, trying to cause the children to feel worn out and prepared to rest. Physical 'crude' play or sports, for example, can turn crazy before bedtime and may make a noisy, loud environment that doesn't prompt feelings of unwinding and preparation for rest. Additionally, if conduct gets wild, a drained parent may respond adversely to the child by yelling and sending them to their room. If the child hits the hay irate, confounded as well as sad, at that point, it is these feelings that will become related to the bedroom, with the impact of expanding any current conduct rest issues. A level of controlled physical effort, for example, a ball game, may enable a few children to free themselves of abundance vitality in status for bed.

Chapter 1:
Mountains of Fun

Once upon a time, there lived twins that loved each other very much. Their names were Alia, and she was very feisty and very adventurous, and Arthur, who was very proud of himself, but also quite cautious. The twins were practically inseparable! They would do everything together! They were also very special twins, for they shared something that was greater than just sharing a birthday; they shared a very special power with each other! It was a very unique power that helped them greatly, for these twins traveled constantly. They were never put in a school the way most children are; rather, these two children spent their time traveling with their parents and doing their schoolwork on the go!

But that is not their power. What is their very special power, though, is the ability to speak to animals! These twins were very good at talking to the animals around them. The animals were always a little surprised to hear a human speaking to them, but they were happy to talk. Some animals would be very kind to the twins; they helped the twins out when they were in trouble. But, other animals did not like the twins much, and they did not like that the twins could talk to them.

No matter where they went, however, the twins knew one thing; they would never be alone so long as they were together and so long as they could continue to speak to animals. After all, animals were everywhere! They were found on the highest peaks of the mountains, and on the desert floor. They knew that, no matter where they went, they could find an animal to talk to; all they would have to do was work hard to find one that would **want** to talk. If they could do that, they could do anything.

One day, Alia and Arthur were brought somewhere new. They were brought to a strange, new mountain range that they had never been to before. It was called the Rocky Mountains, and it went through the United States. Now, the twins were born in the United States, but, they did not spend much time there, as their parents worked very hard as diplomats, going to meet important people in some of the most remote places in the world! But, this time, they were taking a little break. They were there for work, but it was not as busy of work as usual. This time, they were there to meet up with another worker for their company, and that meant that they would get more time than usual with their parents!

This was very exciting for Alia and Arthur, for they loved that very special time with their parents. They loved to be able to walk with them wherever they were going and talk to them without being told, "Hang on; I'm working." And, that very day, they were going to go somewhere very special! They were going to take a hike up the mountain! Alia and Arthur were incredibly happy about this!

So, on the morning of the hike, they all woke up very early, for if you want to be able to complete the whole hike before dark, you have to leave shortly after the sun goes up, and they all got ready to go. Mom packed all sorts of good foods and water. Dad packed lots of sunscreen and bug repellent, and he carried the great, big backpack filled with all of the supplies. Alia and Arthur put on their clothes and their best hiking boots and were ready to go! They could not be more excited to get going than they were right that moment! So, off they ran toward the door, waiting for their parents to follow.

But then, it happened.

The dreaded phone rings. The phone always rang, and their parents would always answer it, and then they'd always have to work. Alia and Arthur looked at each other sadly, knowing what was about to happen. They were very used to being told that things were changing and that they would have to try again another time.

But, that time, the phone was ignored and of they went!

"Where are we hiking to?" asked Arthur, standing next to his father. They were all in a cabin near the bottom of the mountain.

"You see that peak? The one that looks a little funny on the top. We are going to that one," replied his father, looking at a map and a compass.

"Woah, all the way to the top?" asked Alia, peering up at the great, big, blue sky with wide eyes. She didn't' think that she'd be able to climb up that high on her own.

"Only if you want to!" answered their mother.

So, off they all went together on their hike. It was the perfect day for one, too; it was late spring, so it was not yet too hot, but also not too cold to go all the way up the mountain. The sun was shining, and they could not see a single cloud in the sky. They could hear birds chirping their songs everywhere behind them, sounding as beautiful as ever, and the children were very happy that their parents were finally going along with them on one of their nature adventures! Usually, the adventures were just for Alia and Arthur.

But, on this particular adventure, they had to remember something; they were going to be with their parents, and that meant that they could not make use of their very special power. There was to be no talking to any animals at all.

As they all walked together, Alia stopped to look at something, as she loved to do. There was a patch of the most beautiful white wildflowers growing on the side of the trail! It had purple petals that extended out from the center, and white petals surrounding the calyx within them. The flower was very beautiful, and it smelled very nice as well. The smell filled up the air, and it seemed that Alia was not the only one that wanted to stop to smell it. A little bumblebee came buzzing over as well, landing on one of the flowers to suck up some nectar. And, a little further into the patch, Alia could see a hummingbird, dancing through the air. She could hear the soft hum of its tiny wings that flapped faster than any other bird.

Behind her, her mother laughed. "Those are columbine flowers," she said softly. "They are the state flower for Colorado."

"Colorado? Where's that?" Alia asked.

"Here!" answered Arthur. "I think you fell asleep on the plane when we were talking about it. But, we're in the Rocky Mountains in Colorado!

Alia blinked in surprise, but then shrugged her shoulders. "I was tired, okay?" she answered. Then, she heard something— the hummingbird was saying something behind her! It said that it was very tired and very thirsty. But Alia could not speak back, because her parents were there. A quick glance over at Arthur said that he had heard the little hummingbird, too, and he walked over to stand in front of the flower patch, blocking it out of view just right so that their parents could not see what they were about to do. He reached out his hand for the hummingbird, and whispered, as quietly as he could to the bird to land on his hand.

The bird was very surprised to hear a little boy talking, but happily obliged, and Arthur moved the poor tired hummingbird to a branch to stop to rest without it having to fall to the ground. The bird sung it thanks you to the young children and then settled down for a break. So, off they went to keep on exploring all around the mountains.

They traveled even further away than ever—they were looking for something great and new. So, they kept on hiking along the trial. As they hiked, there were some very pretty birds singing in the trees. Alia could hear some chickadees singing in one, and they could see a blue jay in another. They were very happy to see all of the birds that were in the trees around them, and they all sounded very pretty to listen to. But then, they heard something else. They heard a little voice in the distance, crying out, "Help! Help!"

"Do you hear that?" asked the twins' father.

The children looked at him in surprise. Could he hear the animal, too? So, they all followed their father through the big mountain trail. He was leading them somewhere that was very far away, and they left the trail that they had been on, too. They could still hear the crying sounds, and their father still kept on moving forward. Alia and Arthur would look at each other every now and then; they were curious if their father had heard the words too, or if he was only following the sounds of the woods. But there was no way to know for sure unless they asked.

They went up a slope and then turned and went down another way. They went around some big trees and through some trees that were losing all their leaves. They went over a creek, one by one, splashing in the water, and then, they all stopped! They looked around for what they could find around them, and then they saw it—there was a tiny little raccoon with its head stuck in those little plastic rings that are used to hold together cans at the store when they are bought in packs of six!

The raccoon was stuck on the ground, looking very sad, as it had gotten its head stuck on one end, and the other loops, behind him, were stuck to a branch! It could not get out at all on its own, and it would not be able to do anything at all if they did not help it, and quickly! They were going to have to work very hard to get it untangled from the line, but it seemed like the twins' dad had an idea!

He got very close to the raccoon, who continued to cry and ask to be left alone. But then, the twins were very surprised to see that the raccoon stopped! It was looking up at their dad in awe! It looked at him and stopped moving, looking down at the ground, even when their dad picked up his pocketknife and sliced up the plastic! He then quickly pushed the plastic into his own pocket so they would be able to dispose of it themselves and stood up.

They heard the little raccoon squeak out a thank you. And, then, something even more magical happened—their father smiled at it and seemed to nod his own head! Could he hear the raccoon too? They stared up at their father in shock as the raccoon ran away, deeper and deeper into the woods on its own.

Their father, noticing the children staring at him, raised an eyebrow. "What is it?" he asked them curiously, watching as the children seemed very unsure of how they should answer their father.

Alia shook her head. She didn't want to ask! The last time that they had tried to tell someone that they could talk to animals, they thought she was crazy.

But Arthur was braver. "Wow, dad!" he said, very carefully picking out his words. "It was like you were able to talk to that little raccoon to make it stop moving! I've never seen that happen before!" He grinned up at his dad, watching very closely to see if his dad did anything or said anything that would make him doubt that his dad could, in fact, talk to animals just like he could. But, his father did nothing of the sort.

Instead, the twins' father smiled back and patted them on the heads. "You'll understand someday," he said without another word about the subject. "So! It's time for us to finish up our hike, isn't it?"

"Do we have time, dear?" asked their mother, glancing at the sun. It was already more than halfway down; they had spent a lot of their time just looking for the raccoon, and then, helping the raccoon. They weren't upset about it at all, either; they were very happy that they helped save an animal, but it was kind of disappointing to not get to make it to the top of the peak.

"No, I don't think so," he said sadly. "But maybe we can call in tomorrow and schedule another hike! One where we don't get so sidetracked by animals that are in need of help!"

The children looked up longingly at their parents. Getting one day with them was already a pretty big treat—but to get two days in a row? That was almost magical and that was something that almost never happened at all! But, if he could make it happen, they would be more than glad to do so!

So, the family hiked back to their cabin together and spent the evening watching their favorite movies, and the next day, they all spent time hiking right back up the mountain. When they made it all the way to the top, they felt like they were on the top of the world! They could see for miles and miles all around them and it was one of the greatest sights that they had ever seen!

Chapter 2:
Story of the Young Triton

O nce there was a young triton that liked to walk around, visiting all his friends until late in the evening. This kid was now becoming a serious problem, and his parents were getting worried. He was warned about the risky walks to different places around the sea, but he would not listen.

"My son, there are different kinds of animals under the sea, so anytime you move around alone, you risk your life. Are you with me?" his dad told him.

"Yes, dad, I get you very well," the young triton replied.

That night, Kevin went out to bed so early after the long talk from his parents about the dangers around him whenever he walks alone. The undersea world had so many risks, and now that Kevin's dad was the king, everyone would do anything possible just to hurt him. At the same time, his parents were willing to do anything to protect their only son, who was the next in line to the throne of his dad.

"Let's go visit Daniel, then come back," said Kevin's friend.

He had just been told about not going out, but it's like all that fell to a deaf ear. As always, he was just playing outside their home, and then he would disappear and leave with his friend to visit another friend. His parents never noticed the visits, and he thought he was winning. One day, he was playing with his friends. Then the idea of wandering came up; as always, he agreed and left with his friends to go out and play.

"Kevin! It's lunchtime; where are you?" his mother called.

She thought that her son was playing outside the house only to realize that after calling for more than four times, there was no response. Kevin wasn't around, which was something that she knew would not happen. Kevin would always let her know where he is going after the lecture he had been given, so she was sure Kevin was just around. Kevin's mother came out of the house to check what was happening with his son or if he had been sleeping. When she came out of the house, no one was around, and that's when she decided to check at the neighbor's place.

"Have you seen Kevin?" she asked the neighbor.

"They left out in a large group to play," neighbor responded.

Her mother was so angry and felt so bad about Kevin. She thought her son was disrespectful about what they told him and maybe needed to be punished. Kevin, on the other hand, was having so much fun with his friends; everyone was showing their tricks of swimming and how to hunt. His mum went home, furious, waiting for her husband to return so she could report the incident. After some time, the husband came back, and upon hearing the news, he left to find where his son was. The mother was unsettled and just wanted to see her son back home.

The dad was out in the sea, and the mum was in the house when Kevin came back. Her mum couldn't hide the fury in her, so she jumped onto her son and slapped him.

"How many times do we have to tell you that it is perilous outside?" Kevin's mum shouted as she kept on slapping him.

Kevin tried to escape, but her mum had a hold on him so tightly that he couldn't escape. The beatings were so thorough that he could not hold on to his tears. He screamed for help, trying to apologize, but no one could help him. The beatings showed how much her mum was frustrated and, at the same time, worried.

"They were just playing here and left for home," a member of the community told Kevin's dad, who was asking everyone about his whereabouts.

"I don't know what is wrong with this boy; he is not aware of the risks he is putting on him out here," Kevin's dad told himself.

He went straight home, knowing that he would find his son safe from any injuries or harm. Upon reaching home, he had already calmed down and was not furious about what happened. The dad found him crying and embraced him. After some time, it was time for dinner. And as always, the dad had something to tell him after the mistake he had done during the day.

"My son, you have to be respectful of the things we tell you; out there is very dangerous, and you are our only son, so we have to take good care of you and make sure you are always safe. That is why we are strict on you about going out. Do you understand?" said his dad to Kevin.

"Yes, dad, I am sorry I left without getting permission from mum. I won't do it again, and I won't be disrespectful to you," Kevin said to his parents.

That night after dinner, Kevin's parents were left wondering why their son kept on going out, even when it is dangerous in the open sea. After a lot of talks between them, they decided that they will get their son a tutor who will be there to guide their son on what to do. So, the father brought his younger brother home to help look after their son. Kevin felt disappointed during the first days, as this move gave him limitations on where to go. He could spend time sleeping in the house or just swimming around the house because of his uncle, who was always with him and keen on his moves.

His days became so sad, and he could not complain as this was going to lead to either being punished or something severe, which he was not ready to have. He started getting along with his uncle, and this was now going to be an advantage to him, as he would easily convince him to let him go out and play with his friends. The uncle, too, liked him, and their friendship was getting on so well, and with time, they started going out to eat the seafood at the bottom of the sea. This was now a routine they couldn't miss, and Kevin's parents had no issue about it as long as his uncle was with him.

The excursion started becoming so random that the uncle adopted Kevin's ways. They could visit more dangerous places where other animals could eat them, and his dad started getting worried about the trips they were making. Kevin's mum was getting worried, too, and it was getting out of hand that the parents couldn't take it anymore.

"Kevin, we are getting worried about your trips with your uncle; please don't go that far. It's risky, and you may be eaten by other creatures," said Kevin's dad as they listened silently with his uncle.

They had lunch and left for some walk just outside the house. Kevin's dad was getting old, and someone was needed to take over the crown, and that was Kevin. His dad could teach him leadership skills and how to be a good and respected leader. They would go out to the deep sides of the ocean for lessons about good leadership skills. This was the best moment for Kevin as he could be under the protection of the dad and his uncle. He was learning so much daily, and this was a great achievement for him and his dad. The mother, too, was so happy about how his son was doing great when it comes to learning from his dad.

As always, they left for training, and Kevin asked his dad if he could invite his friends to come along. His dad accepted, and Kevin felt so happy about it. His friends got the information, and that afternoon, everyone was ready to go see how skillful Kevin was developing daily. After some preparations, they left for the deep-sea training. The trip was full of learning as Kevin's dad educated the crew about the sea and everything in the sea. The journey was full of questions, thus making it so much fun and educational. They got to the training ground, and his young friends sat aside to watch how Kevin was being trained.

Kevin showed the swimming skills that he had learned, and all his friends cheered for him as he swam swiftly in the sea. His dad was also amused by the progress of his son. The training was going on well until waves started blowing strongly. This was dangerous, as many of the young ones could not swim under such conditions and could be easily washed away. Kevin's dad tried to protect the young kids from the waves, but it was getting rougher that he could not control it. Some of the kids were being carried away, and it was worrying. As they tried to escape from the storm, one of the young ones got washed away and was struggling so much. The whole crew watched pitifully, unable to help. Kevin swam at high speed and risked his life to save his friend. He swam through the waves and could not be seen as he went after his friend. The waves calmed down, and everyone was safe, except for Kevin and his friend. His dad looked worried; he knew his son had died, and he blamed himself for it.

"Kevin! Kevin! Kevin!" his dad called out several times, but there was no response.

He ordered the other kids to go home with the help of his brother while he remained to look for his son. As they were leaving, Kevin came out with his friend, who was also okay. Kevin thanked his dad for the skills he taught him, and the whole neighborhood felt good and happy for his generous act. He was getting ready to be the next leader after his dad, indeed.

Chapter 3:
Paw Island and Coco

Archie left with Maggie and found himself in a magic land. Archie was not willing to take another step unless Maggie explained to him where she was taking him. Archie was right because we should never trust anyone blindly. Sometimes unquestioned truth can lead us to danger. And being careful can help keep us from future danger.

Maggie explained that dogs govern Paw Island. And every dog had some special mission to fulfill and a purpose to serve. The dogs who felt an inner calling were worthy of staying and getting trained on Paw Island. And only the old wizard could decide which dogs were truly righteous. Archie did not believe in the whole thing, but he managed to follow Maggie anyway.

After reaching the wizard's house, Archie learned some startling revelations. The wizard was none other than Paul's lost dog, Coco. Maggie and Coco were very ancient, but they had managed to stay youthful by using special magic to serve their purposes. Archie also came to know about his long-lost siblings. Coco asked Archie to take a test to prove his worthiness. Archie agreed unwillingly, just because he wanted to meet his family.

The test made Archie realized the many problems of having too much anger and hatred. He felt the bliss of helping others. He also came to realize that humans, dogs, and all other creatures were dependent on each other. The best way to live a life was through proper cooperation. The test unburdened him from his hatred. It gave him some relief.

Hating someone cannot harm that person that we hate. But it is harmful to us. Hatred and anger stop us from focusing on good things and the character attributes of others. We spend time hating each other and keeping our right sides veiled. It is okay to feel victimized, but revenge can only lead us to destruction. One hateful act causes us to make another wrong decision, and soon we become drawn into an unbreakable chain of unethical activities. Forgiveness frees us from this vicious cycle. We should always nurture the values we have, such as forgiveness. It frees us from our inner hatred and anger.

Archie had initially trusted Maggie before he set out on his journey. He knew that he did not have any particular destination in mind except possibly to find his siblings one day. He was lost and clueless about his life. He had known Maggie for only two days. And Maggie surprisingly had convinced him to start a journey towards the unknown and she had brought him to a strange land called 'Paw Island.' After crossing the entrance, they saw a lovely city with no trace of humans. Archie was beyond astonished and completely delighted. For some time, Archie thought he must be dreaming because what he was observing was illogical and irrational. Maggie was still maintaining her calmness and composure, which meant this was not the first time Maggie had been here in this weird place.

Archie finally broke his silence and asked, "Don't you think I deserve some explanation about this place?"

Maggie's reply was vague. "You really have some serious trust issues. Have I done anything wrong or harmful to you yet?"

Archie hated twisted and cynical answers. And above all, he had no reason to trust Maggie blindly. He said, "I want to trust you. But trust is something that needs to be earned. You are not pushing me in front of a car or leaving me alone, because that is the right gesture of any sane person. That does not mean I will blindly trust you, whatever you say. And there is a difference between trust and blind trust. Having blind trust is never a wise decision to make."

Maggie knew that Archie was right, and he deserved the truth. Maggie said, "This is Paw Island. You already know the name. This is the paw world. We have our schools, universities, community centers, a special training center, and everything a civilized society needs. Everything is run by Dogs only. This is a special dog land where dogs like you and me can feel safe. We all have a mission. We are gate-trained here, and then we enter the human world in order to fulfill our missions."

Archie listened to every word carefully but hardly understood anything. He had never heard of it. If dogs already had a special land, then why would they choose to be the lapdog of others? This was a lot to believe and understand. Eating thrown-out food and crossing a road full of cars were much easier to accept than this. Maggie was not older than Archie - she was just a puppy like him. She had been living a good life in that house, cuddling with Izzy. If she had already known about Paw Island, then why would she have been living with Izzy? Now she was talking about some secret mission - how was that even possible? Either she was lying, or this entire thing was a bad dream!

Maggie was waiting for Archie to ask questions. She knew that understanding this whole situation was a bit challenging for Archie. Even worse, Archie had a choice - he could run away from here. But Archie did nothing like that. He just stood still, totally silent, because he did not know what questions to ask her. Finally, Maggie could wait no longer. She asked, "Do you want to know more? Don't you have anything to ask me? I think you have finally got your home."

Archie shook his head in disagreement and replied, "Look, Maggie, I appreciate your help. I know that you want to help me and have sympathy for me because of my past and all, but that doesn't give you the right to play sick games with me. Yes, I have something to ask. Who gave you the right to mess with my brain? I am feeling lost for now, but why you have misguided me?!"

Maggie had thought that Archie would be happy. She had not been expecting this reaction, but she also knew that this revelation was intimidating, as well. So, she tried to convince him again. She said, "I have already told you that I do not have any sympathy for you because you are my friend, and that is why I am willing to help you. I also know that this is hard to believe - what I am telling you it is beyond your imagination. My secret mission is to bring people like you to this island. I am very old, but I always keep looking tiny due to magic. It helps me to keep doing my job and fulfill my mission, and Izzy's home was not the first home where I lived with a family. I keep changing families to search for worthy puppies like you who feel that they have some purpose in life to serve, or that there is a hole in their life. Our wisest wizard decides whom to keep and train here." She waited for a reply, but there was none.

Maggie continued, "I know that I have not given you the chance to trust me blindly, but I did not ruin your beliefs either. I am just asking you to follow me for some time, and then to go with me to see the wizard. You can *have* all the answers you have been seeking for so long," Maggie continued.

Archie was unsure, but there was a sincerity in her voice. She deserved another chance, so Archie replied, "Ok. I will come with you, but I have one condition. If I feel that this whole thing is nothing, but a hoax and your old wise Wizard is nothing but a con artist, then I will leave immediately, and you will not be able to stop me, or try to convince me, either. You will help me to get out of this hocus-pocus land. Deal!"

Maggie knew one thing about Archie - arguing with him would never end well. Archie was a stubborn one. He would not go one step further without making that deal. So, Maggie nodded in agreement. All the dogs of Paw Island were busy doing their everyday chores, and no one was paying attention to the new puppy roaming around with Maggie. Maggie and Archie came in front of an ancient Castle. Dogwood trees surrounded the castle. The castle was made of stones, and old creepers were everywhere on its outer wall. The island was covered with snow, and everyone was getting ready for Christmas. Even the Castle was being decorated for Christmas. Archie saw that the wreaths on the door were made of bone-shaped wooden artifacts instead of dry flowers. They noticed the door was half shut. Maggie walked towards the door and knocked softly. An ancient and wrinkled dog opened the door. There was a serene smile on his face, and he looked at Archie eagerly, as if he had been expecting him for a long time.

Maggie bowed down in front of the old dog, but Archie did not feel the urge to do anything. He had no reason to be respectful, but he *was* intrigued by the wizard's expression. The wizard asked, "Dear child, who is our guest today? And what took you so long in bringing him here?"

Maggie was also perplexed by the wizard's manner, but she managed to gather herself together. She replied, "Wizard, most of the dogs are happy and comfortable with their present domestic lives. They are getting enough food, a warm place to sleep, and walks around clean parks. No one is feeling the urge to be better, or to do something for others. They are not willing to give back to this society, or to humans, or even to us. They are contented. After a long time, I met him; his name is Archie. He feels that he has some mission; he is aimless but feels that he has some purpose. He was ready to leave all the comforts behind him without any attachment. He was ready to start his journey to get his answer."

The wizard smiled and said, "I see. So, Archie, may I give you a test to see whether you are worthy or not? But, before that, tell me - how are you feeling?"

Archie had expected an elaborate introductory speech on how to be worthy and why to help others. But the wizard preferred to stay on point. Archie replied, "Ok. Before you give me some weird test, is it ok if I ask you something? Maggie had told me that you have some magical power or something, and you are very ancient. If that is true, then why are you all wrinkled? Why are you not magically changing yourself into a young dog? And I cannot call you Wizard, so I guess you must have a name!?"

The wizard smiled and said, "You are wise. You know what to ask and when to ask it. I do not bother to use magic to stay young anymore because I have not taken any missions in the outer world for some time. One thing is clear from this conversation, though - you do not believe anything blindly, and that is a great virtue. We should always ask questions until we feel that there is nothing left to ask. Curiosity leads us to wisdom, child. I am not transforming myself into a younger-looking dog because I don't feel the need. Maggie needs to stay young because she needs to stay with families. And no one is willing to take responsibility for an old and feeble dog. It doesn't matter whether I am very young or very old looking; wisdom is everything for me. If you are wise, then being beautiful or being ugly doesn't matter. People will always respect you and come to you for your suggestions. I have a name, and my name is Coco!"

Archie was shocked to know the name. He asked, "Coco! Are you Paul's Coco? You were lost, and he still misses you. If you are wise and all, then why did you leave that house? I think they are good people. And you said you no longer go in the outer world, but if you are that Coco, then this whole thing does not make any sense."

Wizard coco's smile became broader. Archie had the qualities to be able to connect all the dots. He replied, "You are right; I am Paul's Coco. You see, on Paw Island, we are all driven by some mission, and we are bound to fulfill that. No matter how we feel about it, we have to come back to this land after fulfilling every mission. Three years ago, I had envisioned a prophecy that a wise puppy was about to born. And one family helped him to reach us. I had to make sure that the family was kind enough to take care of that prophesied puppy. So, I went there and lived with them for some time. When I became satisfied, I had to leave. I think you know who that prophesied dog is. I have lived here for 12 lifetimes. And I can live fourteen lifetimes in total. Archie, you are supposed to be the next wizard of Paw Island. But that's a long way to go. Tell me, why did you feel the urge to leave all the comforts behind?

Archie was still processing everything, and he was silent. He thought, 'These people are mad. How can I turn into a wizard? Are they lying to me?' But he did not utter anything and instead replied absentmindedly, "I was not at all comfortable there. I hate humans. They are rude and unkind. Paul and his family were kind to me, but that does not mean I trust them. Living inside a comfortable house can never satisfy me. I started my journey to find out my siblings, especially my little sister Katty. But then I realized I have no idea where to find her. I stayed on the road for one night. Then Paul took me in."

Coco smiled mysteriously. "If I say that living on-road and meeting Tobby was part of our bigger plan, will you believe me?"

"I think I can believe anything you say at this point. Because you already know Tobby's name and I am guessing he was also part of some secret mission. I still do not know what I am doing here. And why should I be the next wizard of Paw Island?" Archie asked.

Coco requested that Maggie leave them alone. Maggie knew that her job was done here for now, so she said goodbye and left. Coco said, "Katty lives here with us, and all your siblings are here, too, because your parents were senior ministers of this land. Your bloodline has been serving the missions of Paw Island for many generations now. And I know that one day you will also feel the same urge to do so. And I know you have a trust issue. You do not need to trust me unless I prove myself worthy of your trust. But you need to know one thing. I am your great-great-great grandfather. Now it is time for your test."

Not so long ago, Archie had nothing. He was all alone, with no family and no one to depend on. And now he was standing in front of his heretofore unknown great-great-great grandfather. He could not say anything, and he was choked up. He knew that, in spite of his being family, Coco would never let him meet his siblings before this stupid test. So, he agreed.

Coco took him to a room full of antiques and talismans. There was a crystal globe in the center of the room. Coco asked Archie to focus on that globe. Archie concentrated on the globe, but nothing was happening. He was still standing with Coco, inside that room. After some time, Coco requested that he stop concentrating and go outside for some air. Archie was confused about this whole testing process. He still did not know what the test was. Nothing happened at all.

When he came out, he saw there was a gate in front of Wizard's house. He had not noticed the entrance before. But the gate was not important because he was lost in thought. He was still thinking about all the information he had to digest. How could this wizard be his great-great-great grandfather? How could his siblings be in this weird place? He absentmindedly crossed through the gate. Suddenly he heard a loud noise. He found himself standing beside a road. The road was being repaired, and a lot of people were working.

Archie gathered himself and noticed what was going on around him. He was no longer in Paw Island. He was in the city and standing in front of an under-construction building. A crane had lost its control and banged a wall. Now it was trying to pull itself up, as its one part was stuck in the mud.

He noticed a blind schoolboy was walking alone towards the crane. No one noticed him because everyone was busy pulling the crane up. Archie realized if the boy kept walking in that direction, he would be severely injured.

Archie ran towards the boy and began to bark loudly. He reached the boy in no time and grabbed the boy's umbrella with his teeth. Then, he started pulling the boy with all his might. The boy followed Archie's lead and finally reached a safe area, away from the construction site. Archie had saved the boy's life.

This was the first time Archie felt the magic of real bliss, a bliss of saving someone's life. He had never felt that before. Archie realized why Paul had helped him, and why people supported and helped one another. No matter how much Archie had believed he hated humans, he could not let that boy get hurt. Every creature on earth needs help from the other ones. And to survive, we should all live together and support each other. Archie felt like a veil was lifted from his eyes; he had been blind in his rage. He also felt like a burden had been lifted from his heart. He was relieved. Hatred could not give him anything besides pain. He realized that instantly. Archie sighed and closed his eyes to relish the moment.

When he opened his eyes, he found himself in Coco's room. His test was complete. Archie had learned a simple truth of life. He was worthy. He was ready to be trained for his mission for the greater good.

Chapter 4:
An Orphan

O nce upon a time, there was a student living in an orphanage. His name was Alex. His parents had died in an accident when he was too young. There was no one to look after him, his uncle leaves him to the orphanage. He raised in an orphanage. He always thought where his parents had gone and left him alone, but as time passes, he became used to, to live there. he likes to explore new things. He always feels alone and has not many friends.

One day he decided to go out from orphanage to explore the world. He never goes outside. But there was no permission to go outside. He decided to go out when everyone would be sleeping. He went out of the room at night to check whether everyone is sleeping. When no one was there, then he unlocked the door slightly and went outside. He used to jump over the orphanage's boundary wall and roam around. So, he jumped over the wall.

He saw shops which were closed and no traffic on the road because he went outside at mid of night. He has to return back to the orphanage before dawn. He roamed here and there and got afraid because the night was dark. He had to return. He jumped over the boundary wall of the orphanage and slowly moved to his room without making any noise and get back to sleep.

The next day he again decided to go outside with courage, then he again climbed to the boundary wall of the orphanage and jumped outside. He walked two miles. There he saw a boy sitting alone on the road. He went close to him and asked him "why are you sitting here alone, and what is your name?" The boy replied, "My name is Sam, and this is the place I live". He told him that his mother had died 4 days before. And there was no one who looked after him and gave food to him.

Alex said, "why won't you come with me, I'm also an orphan and my parents have died in an accident". The boy agreed to go with him. He said, "I have not taken permission from Father to go outside". Alex said "you should come to the orphanage tomorrow. And we will meet tomorrow at the orphanage". The boy replied, "ok". Alex said, "I'm getting late I should go now". The sun rises. Alex runs speedily back to the orphanage and goes to his room.

The day arises the boy came to the church and told the Father about his mother and all situations he faced. The Father decided to take that child to the orphanage. Then in the evening, he met Alex. They both became good friends. They played together, ate together, studied together. Alex said to Sam that he again wanted to go outside and explore things.

At night they both jumped over the boundary wall of the orphanage and go outside. There Sam takes Alex to the park where they play games and then they decided to go three miles far where they found a fruit shop which was opened late at night. They became hungry. And go to that shop and asked the shop keeper to give them one apple, but they have no money the shopkeeper refuses to give them an apple. The sun was about to rise. They decided to go back to the orphanage.

The next day Sam refuses to go with Alex because he realizes that it is not a good thing to go outside without taking permission from Father. But Alex said I'm getting tired from this place I want to see the world. Alex decided to go out alone. And that night father was awake, and he had seen Alex going out. He got up to stop him, but he was gone. After a few hours later when he gets back to the orphanage, he opened the door and he saw Father was looking at him.

He became scared. But Father told him that "son, at least you should take a warm shawl, because you know when you go at night, it is cold outside." Fathers gentle manner made Alex realize his own folly. He feels ashamed and guilty. He apologized to the Father and promised him that he would never go outside without taking permission from him.

Chapter 5:
Hailey Goes on a Nature Walk

Hailey loved nature and everything about the outdoors. When she was just a baby, her mom used to strap her to a baby carrier and carry Hailey along some of the coolest hikes in the Pacific North West.

They would climb mountains, scale trails, and check out incredible waterfalls that decorated the sides of the cliffs they hiked near.

As she got older, Hailey was able to start walking the trails herself, and soon, it became her favorite hobby.

Hailey loved getting to see the outdoors and all of the curious wonders of the world when she was out in nature, so much so that she was always asking to go on nature hikes with her mom.

One day, Hailey realized they had not been on a nature hike in a while.

Life had been busy for her mom, and she had not been able to make much time for the two of them to do anything together.

Hailey felt sad and wanted to go on a walk, so she asked her mom if they could go soon.

Hailey's mom said yes, and the two went for a nature walk that very next weekend.

At first, Hailey was surprised because they did not get in the car to go anywhere.

When they went on hikes, Hailey's mom would always pack the car, and they would drive away to the trail and then do their hike.

This time, Hailey's mom never packed anything, and they never got into the car.

Instead, they put on their shoes and their sweaters and started walking down the road.

"Where are we going?" Hailey asked, following her mom down the road.

"On a nature walk." Hailey's mom answered.

"Where?" Hailey asked.

"You'll see!" Hailey's mom said.

Confused, Hailey kept walking with her mom down the road.

At first, she had no idea what was going on.

Then, Hailey grew frustrated and angry with her mom.

This is not what she wanted; Hailey wanted to go on a nature walk, not a walk down the road.

What was her mom thinking? Hailey wondered.

"This suck, I want to go home!" Hailey said, growing annoyed with their walk.

By now, they had turned several corners, but they were still just on the road; there was not a trail to be found.

"Just wait, Hailey, be patient, please. You will see what we are doing." Hailey's mom answered, continuing to walk.

Hailey reluctantly followed, although by now, she was not having any fun.

She wanted to go home and play with her toys and pretend this day had never happened.

All she wanted was to go on a nature walk with her mom, and instead, they were walking around the neighborhood, and she had no idea where they were going.

After a few more turns, Hailey's mom turned into a small trail that opened up into a field.

"We're here!" she said, looking around.

Still confused, Hailey looked around at where they were.

They had made their way to one of the local parks.

"Where?" Hailey asked.

"On a nature walk, silly!" Hailey's mom smiled.

"This is not a nature walk, mom, this is a park," Hailey said, matter of fact.

"Oh, really? Well, then, what is this!" Hailey's mom said, pointing to a strange plant that lined the trails.

Hailey rolled her eyes at her mom and then looked closer.

As she looked, she realized the plant was unlike anything she saw before.

It's purple-black leaves curled in every which direction and had tiny hairs on them that made it look like they were little hairy plant hands reaching up for sunlight.

Hailey giggled and stood back up.

"Okay, cool plant. But what now?" Hailey asked.

"Do you hear that?" Hailey's mom asked.

"Hear what?" "That sound, that bird!" Hailey's mom said.

"Yes, I do!" Hailey answered, starting to get excited about the park they were in.

"Let's go find it!" Hailey's mom said.

The two of them began walking toward where the sound was coming from.

As they followed the path, they came across the bird that was up in a tree chirping at them.

It was a red-crested woodpecker, calling to his friends before pecking the side of a tree to get a meal.

"Cool!" Hailey said, watching him as he called and then pecked the side of the tree.

Hailey and her mom started walking down the path through the park a little further, and as they did, they started seeing several different types of plants and birds all around them.

Then, they started seeing cool bugs.

First, Hailey saw a fancy spider that was spinning its web.

Then, she saw a little caterpillar chewing on a leaf.

As they kept walking, they also saw a beaver in the nearby creek, three more spiders, a ladybug, two grasshoppers, and several bumblebees.

Hailey started counting out all of the different things she saw as they walked around the park.

Her mom also stopped to take a few pictures of the birds and the beautiful plants that were all around the park they were in.

When they got to the end of the trail, they made their way back to the street.

Hailey was sure the nature walk was over and started to feel sad again, but her mom assured her there was plenty more to see.

"There is so much nature in our own back yard!" Hailey's mom grinned, pointing out several different plants, bugs, and birds along the way.

Hailey continued looking for cool species that were all around their walk.

She was surprised to realize that there were so many cool things to see in their own neighborhood.

In the past, she only noticed the houses, driveways, and cars.

But now, she could see that her own neighborhood had so many incredible pieces of nature woven into it.

She knew that she would never see her own neighborhood the same way again.

As they approached their home, Hailey's mom asked her if she enjoyed the nature walk, they had.

"I did!" Hailey's smiled.

"I wished we were going on a nature hike because I wanted to go see a waterfall or a mountain, but this was a really fun walk, too. Thank you for taking me, mom." Hailey said.

"I know you wanted to go on a hike, Hailey, but sometimes life gets busy, and we cannot go do things like that. I know you are disappointed, but I am grateful that you are so kind about it. If you are patient for just a little bit longer, everything at work will settle down, and we will be able to go on a real hike again real soon. Until then, I hope you are ok with us just going on nature walks around our own neighborhood. There are so many cool things to see here, too!" her mom said.

"I am sad we didn't go, but I know. It was a fun walk. I did not know we had so many things in our own neighborhood!" Hailey said.

"Me neither." her mom smiled, hugging her.

When they were done talking, Hailey's mom got them both a cup of juice and some snacks to help fill their bellies after a long walk.

The two enjoyed their juice and snacks and talked about all of the cool things they saw, and about what they hoped to see when they went for another walk the following weekend.

And, when things got more calm at work, Hailey's mom took her on a hike as she promised, and they both got to enjoy a wonderful trip together watching waterfalls falling down cliffs and seeing mountains rising high into the sky.

Chapter 6:
Dino Chef and the Great Soufflé

D ino puttered around the kitchen, gathering some of the tools and ingredients he would need for his next project. He picked up some flour, some eggs, a bowl, a whisk, and a measuring cup. He set them down on the counter and laid them out neatly so he could get to work.

"Today, I'm going to make a soufflé! It's a light and fluffy dessert that tastes so sweet and yummy, and it's so light and fluffy that only the best chefs can get them right every single time!"

Dino spun one of the eggs in a little circle on the countertop as he thumbed through his cookbook for the perfect soufflé recipe. When he found the page, he set the book down and studied the instructions carefully.

"It says here that I will need to make sure the oven is preheated to exactly the right temperature, and that I will need some baking dishes." Dino hurried around the kitchen, preparing everything for his delicious soufflé.

"I've made stew, I've made pizza, I've made **lots** of pasta, and I've even made my own pies! I'll bet that a great chef like me can make the perfect soufflé on the very first try!" Dino hummed to himself as he followed the directions in his cookbook.

Finally, Dino was ready to put his creation into the oven to bake. Just some patient waiting and there would be a delicious dessert waiting for him at the end of it.

Dino set the timer as he sat down in a chair he had in the kitchen. He picked up a book, kicked up his feet, and read while he waited for the timer to go off. Soufflés take a long time to bake, so Dino was sure he could finish his book by the time it was done!

Sometime later, when the timer was ticking down its last minutes, Dino had forgotten all about his book and was staring into the oven through the little window on the front. The soufflé looked like it was getting nice and fluffy on top! It almost looked like a giant muffin in its big dish.

The timer dinged and Dino flung open the door to the oven, slapped mitts on his hands, and took the delicious dessert out of the oven. He held up the dish, admiring the golden sweet fluff in front of him. Happily, he set down the soufflé, shut the door to the oven, turned off the heat, and turned around.

To Dino's horror, the soufflé had caved in on itself when his back was turned! Dino panicked as he watched all the air seep out of his fluffy dessert. Soon, the top of the dessert settled in near the bottom of the dish, leaving nothing behind but a sweet crater in the center of the bowl.

Dino paused for a moment, looking at the dish and the dessert he has been working on all afternoon. Soon, tears filled his eyes and he put his head down on the counter to cry.

"I just wanted to make the most delicious soufflé that ever was! I followed all the directions perfectly and it looked so beautiful when I took it out of the oven." Dino cried and cried. He read the directions for the soufflé recipe once again, to make sure that he hadn't missed anything when he was making it. He couldn't find anywhere that he had gone wrong.

Dino sat up and wiped his tears. He looked down at his flattened soufflé and then looked back at the cookbook. With a spoon from his drawer, Dino took a small piece of the soufflé and tasted it. His mouth closed around the spoon and his eyes glittered, his cheeks blushed, and his spirits soared. It was an absolutely **delicious** dessert and Dino was so proud of it.

"How could something this delicious still be wrong?" Dino asked himself. He continued to eat the soufflé as he read through the directions. "I know! This means that I've almost got it right. The flavor is perfect, all the ingredients are right, I just have to fix the way it puffs up. I can make a better one!" Dino zipped around the kitchen, picking up everything he would need in order to make another soufflé.

Carefully, he put all his ingredients together in just the right way. He got everything ready to go, he popped the soufflé into the oven, and he set his timer. Once again, Dino sat down in the kitchen with his book. This time, he was sure he would finish the book. Things were just starting to get really good in the story and he couldn't wait to see how it ended!

Sometime later, the kitchen timer was just about to go off and Dino had once again completely forgotten all about his book. He hopped around the kitchen, from foot to foot, waiting for the timer to go off so he could look at his creation. He just knew that this time, he would get everything right and it would look just as great as it tasted.

Finally, the timer sounded, and Dino pulled the oven door open. He carefully pulled the soufflé from the oven and set it down on the counter as gently as he could. He switched off the oven and closed the door, all without taking his eyes off of the soufflé. Slowly, he took off his oven mitts and put them back in their place, never looking away from his dessert. When he was done, he put his hands on his hips and stood in front of the soufflé. He let out a relieved sigh and said, "I think I got it this time!" He closed his eyes and threw his hands in the air.

Just as he looked away, as though the soufflé heard what he said, it caved in on itself, forcing all the air out of it. Dino flopped onto the floor and sat, looking up at the dish on the counter.

"Well isn't that just... SOMETHING. What am I missing with my soufflé? Something must be wrong.

Dino hopped back up onto his feet and grabbed the oven mitts once more. He grabbed the baking dish and put it into his bag with some foil on top. He raced out to his Vespa and drove straight to the bakery where Pietro was getting ready to lock up for the evening.

"Pietro! I need your help with my latest creation. Do you have some time?" Pietro, whose key was in the lock to his bakery, unlocked the door once more and gestured for Dino to go inside.

"I always have time to help a friend! What can I help you with, Dino?"

"Thank you so much for being here, Pietro." Dino slipped the mitts back onto his dinosaur claws and pulled the soufflé out of the bag. He set it on the counter and pulled the foil off of it. "This is the second one I've made, and it won't stop falling apart like this! Can you tell me what I'm doing wrong?"

"A-ha! I already know the answer, just by looking at it. It's too dry."

"Dry?" Dino asked. "But it's so delicious. There's nothing dry about it when I eat it.

"Well the **inside** is moist, but the outside is too dry and the crust up at the top is too dry to hold a shape, so its **frump** falls in on itself." Dino looked at the soufflé and poked at the top of it with his claw, noticing that it was a bit dry.

"How do I fix it? I followed the recipe in my book exactly. Should I add more milk?"

"Absolutely not." Pietro stepped forward and grabbed one of the spoons from the counter. He tasted the soufflé. "It's perfect inside. What you must do is bake a dish full of water along with your soufflé. When you bake the soufflé, it will have all that water in the air around it, keeping it fluffy and perfect."

"That is pure genius, Pietro! I will try that. Thank you so much!" Dino put his mitts back on, grabbed his soufflé, and ran right back out the door. He would get this soufflé right, even if it took the whole night long! He got back up on his Vespa and drove back to his kitchen.

When he arrived, he threw all the ingredients together with no problem. When you have to make a recipe so many times, you start to remember all the steps without reading the book!

Dino placed a large baking pan filled with water into the oven and placed his soufflé dish right into the center of it. Once more, he set his timer. He looked at his book on the table and sighed. There was no way he could give the book the attention it needed. Even if he did finish the book now, he wouldn't be able to take it all in.

Dino laid on the floor of the kitchen and listened to his little timer ticking away the seconds until his soufflé was ready to be pulled out of the oven. He thought about the soufflé and how delicious it would be when he finally got it right. His tired eyes started to see little smiling soufflés dancing around before he dozed off, right on the kitchen floor.

Sometime later, Dino woke up to the ringing of his kitchen timer. It was time! The soufflé was cooked, and this was the moment of truth. He hopped up, turned off the oven, slipped the mitts onto his hands, opened the oven, and pulled out the beautiful, golden soufflé. Little swirls of steam curled up off of the dessert as he carefully placed it on the counter and admired its beautiful, strong shape.

He closed the oven, he turned it off once more, and he stood in front of the soufflé, watching it carefully. He walked around the kitchen, keeping his eye on it. He walked to another part of the kitchen and he kept looking at the soufflé. Carefully, he closed his eyes. When he opened them, he looked back up at the soufflé that sat there peacefully, billowing more sweet steam.

Dino smiled and, just as he was about to run over to look at it closely, he stopped himself. He walked over to the refrigerator and opened the door. He stood behind it, so his view of the soufflé was blocked. Slowly, he peeked out from behind the door, to see the soufflé sitting there, just as perfect as when he had pulled it out of the oven.

He walked to the door of the kitchen and pushed it open slowly. He walked out, looking cautiously at the soufflé. The door closed behind him and in an instant, he burst back through it to try to catch the soufflé deflating once again. But the soufflé didn't change! It sat on the counter, looking fluffy.

He knelt on his hands and knees and crawled over to the counter to sneak up on the soufflé. Just when the soufflé wouldn't be suspecting him, he jumped up and made a big dinosaur roar! But the soufflé stayed perfect!

Dino had finally done it! He had made a delicious soufflé that looked just as beautiful as the one in his cookbook! Dino walked to the middle of his kitchen and did a little victory dance. He wiggled his tail from side to side, he kicked his feet out to either side and pumped his fists.

"Dino is the greatest chef who ever was! This soufflé is the best thing ever and I have done something amazing in my kitchen today!" Dino kept dancing as he cleaned up the kitchen. He wiped down all the counters, he emptied his pan of water, he washed all his utensils, and he looked back at his perfect soufflé from time to time to keep his dancing going.

When he was all done, Dino fixed himself a little bit of dinner and sat down at the table to eat. He finished his food and he sat down with a nice piece of soufflé and his book. Now, he could finish the book, he would know what happened in the end, and he could pay attention now that he wasn't worried about making the most perfect soufflé!

What a wonderful way to spend an evening.

Chapter 7:
Leopard and the four kids

O nce upon a time, there was a Goat who after giving birth to her four kids died. They were left to take care of themselves.

All of them left their mother and they had to fend for themselves. At first, they were all walking together but later, they went on their separate ways.

As one of the kids kept walking on his own, he came across a leopard. The Leopard quickly went to him and made friends with him. The Leopard began to ask him questions and he told him that they are four but that they have separated and that he is in search of food. The Leopard quickly said to himself: "These kids won't be bad for food". He then told the kid that he should follow him and that he has food for him. He took him to his house and asked him to enter so that he can give him food. As soon as he entered, he pounced on him and ate him. When he finished eating him, he made up his mind to also go looking for the other ones and kill them.

The second kid also continued in his search for food. As he was walking, whatever he saw on the road, he ate. Before long, he met the Leopard who quickly made friends with him. "Hello, it seems you are new around" here says Leopard. He also responded and said, "Hi, yes, I am new here". What brought you to town asked the leopard. The kid went ahead to explain what happened to their mother and how they all separated to go and look for food. Leopard then asked him if he had a house and he said no and that he has just been sleeping around. He then offered him his house. With joy, the kid followed him. When they got to his house, he told the kid to make himself comfortable as he has nothing to be afraid of. He even gave him lunch. They talked and talked. When night came, he pounced on the kid and though, the kid begged him not to kill him, but he didn't answer, he killed and ate him immediately.

The third kid decided to build a house because he thought within himself that if he can build a house, he will not be attacked by wild animals and he will also have a place to rest. He went ahead to get all the materials needed and he then started building. When he was almost done, the leopard saw him carrying something so heavy and he exclaimed, " Why didn't you call for help? This is quite big for you". He then offered to help him. He helped him carry the material and when they got home, he assisted him in the building. The kid thanked him for helping out and asked to know where he was living. He then told the kid that he is trying to fix some things in his house and so, he is not sleeping at home that night. He said he was on his way to his friend's house when he saw the kid. The kid felt so sorry for him and asked him to move in with for as long as he wants. They both ate and slept.

Leopard began to stay with him. After a few days, when they were sleeping in the night, the leopard woke up and saw his friend sleeping. He killed him and ate him. When he was done eating, he left the house and went away.

The fourth kid decided to build a very strong house and then, stock it with enough food so that when he is inside, he will be safe from danger. He got all the material needed and took his time to build it.

Then came the Leopard again, as he got to the fourth kid's house, he called to him "Oh dear Goat, let me come in and stay with you till dawn. My house is very far from here and I need a place to stay until tomorrow."

The Goat answered him from inside, "No, my dear Leopard, you have no place here. I don't want any visitor."

"I will pull down your house and come in. I will then feast on you", the Leopard said. "You can try your luck", the Goat replied.

Well, he tried everything, but he could not pull down the house. When he found that he could not, he was disappointed and angry at the same time and he made up his mind to do everything within his power to get the kid. He left and came back again at another time.

A few days after, he came to the kid's house and called out again, "Nice structure you've got here, kid. I need to build something as strong as this. Can you allow me in to take a look at the inside?" The kid replied to him from inside, "Well, Leopard, the way the outside is, is the way the inside is. You don't need to come in". The Leopard was angrier this time around and told himself that when next he comes; he is going to break the roof of the kid's house and kill him.

He came again after some days. As he got outside, he called out, "My friend, I am here again to give you a gift. Just come out and accept my token of love for you". The kid replied him from inside and said, "Oh thank you, that's quite thoughtful of you, I am coming." The Leopard was happy that at last, he is going to get him but unknown to him, the kid had kept a dagger by the window to use to kill him. Suddenly, the kid opened his window and threw the dagger, it hit the Leopard on the head, and he fell.

The kid then came down and killed it. He boiled him and ate him. He then lived in peace ever after.

Chapter 8:
The Forest Boy and
The Shepherd Girl

O nce upon a time, there was a boy who grew up in the forest. The forest trees and flowers were his friends. They sang different songs to him. Sometimes, if he offends one of them, while others are singing for him, the one he offended will be saying bad things about him. He had never lived outside the forest. He ate and slept there. By himself, he will play with all the flowers and trees, they will also laugh and clap with him. He never thought there was another life outside the forest.

One day, as he was walking inside the forest, he saw some people and he decided to follow them. He kept following them from a distance. He was very surprised to see that there is a village not too far from where he lived. He has never seen humans before, so, he was surprised to see people. He saw their market and heard them buying and selling. He was moving from one place to another and he loved what he saw. After spending some time there, he made up his mind to come there sometimes. Day after day, he was coming to the market to see people. His friends in the forest were always missing him whenever he leaves them but whenever he is back, they kept singing for him.

One day, when he got to the market, he saw a woman selling flowers and saw that many people were buying. He was so surprised and then, he thought to himself that there are even more beautiful flowers from where he is coming. He then decided to come and be selling flowers in the market. When he got to the forest, he told the flowers what happened at the market and that he wants to be selling flowers. The flowers told him to go ahead and cut from them. He was very happy.

On the market day, he got up early and got plenty of flowers and carried it to the market. As soon as he got to the market, the villagers were fascinated by the scent of the flowers. As they were so beautiful, and for each of his flowers, he received a gold coin. Many villagers came to buy from him as they had never seen flowers so beautiful as that. He made plenty of money that day and as he got to the forest, he went straight to the flowers and told them what happened at the market and the plenty of money he made. They were so happy. They sang for him and also told him she can always come and pick from them.

He was always going to the market frequently and he was making a lot of money as many people were buying the flowers because they were very beautiful, much more than the ones they've always seen. One day, when he got to the market, he saw a shepherd boy who came to meet him to buy flowers. As the boy got to him, he smiled at him and greeted, the boy loved him immediately. That was how they became friends.

Whenever he is done selling every day, the shepherd boy will see him off and after some time, turn back while he continues his journey into the forest. Each day, they look forward to seeing each other.

One day, after he finished selling flowers, he carried his container and money, as he was about leaving the market, the shepherd boy came with his sister to say hi to his newfound friend. He quickly made friends with the girl and that was how the three of them started meeting at the market square. When the shepherd boy and girl are done tending the sheep, they would come to the market square to see their friend. When he finishes selling, they will see him off and go back after some time.

The flowers in the forest continued to sing for him whenever he comes back from the market. They were his friends in the forest. He started liking the shepherd girl. One day, he decided to take the most beautiful of the flowers and give them to the girl. Before cutting it, he told the flower, "In this forest, you are the one I love most. May I give you to the girl I love?". The flower said, "Yes, go ahead". He thanked the flower and went ahead to pick a few of the flowers. When his friends came visiting, he gave the girl the special flower as a symbol of his love for her. The girl was very happy, and she thanked him.

Both of them began to plan on getting married and he agreed to leave the forest and come and stay in the village with the girl.

When he got to the forest, he spoke to the trees and flowers. He thanked them for being his friends for years and how they have kept him company all the while. He told them about the girl he wants to marry and how much he loves him and that he wants to start living in the village after marrying her. All of them began to talk about how much they are going to miss him. One of the trees then said, "You have made so much money from selling flowers, use that money to build a house for yourself and the girl". All of them chorused, "That's a good idea". A flower also told him, "You can continue to sell your flowers. Come and be plucking us and we will keep increasing for you to get more every day". All of them agreed. He then thanked all of them for their support. They asked him to bring the girl so that they can do a farewell party for him when she comes.

He began to build the house in the village and when he finished, he brought the girl to the forest. All the trees and flowers sang many beautiful songs for both of them. The farewell party was great. When they finished, both of them left the forest and the boy and girl lived happily ever after.

Chapter 9:
The Luck Dragon

O nce upon a time, a boy named Matthew was lucky enough to travel all the way to China, half the world away from where he lived in the United States. His mom had to attend a business conference there—she worked for a large technology company—and decided to allow Matthew to tag along. There would be children of other businesspeople there, therefore, she thought it would be nice for Matthew to meet some new friends and experience some new cultural encounters. The timing of the conference happened to coincide with the celebration of Chinese New Year, or Lunar New Year - one of the biggest celebrations in China at any time of the year. Matthew was, needless to say, so excited he couldn't sleep the night before they left.

After a really, really long flight—truly, Matthew couldn't believe that he could sit on a plane for that many hours—they landed in Beijing, the big gray capital of China, home to millions and millions of people. Once they got their things settled in the hotel room, Matthew's mom and their guide took him around the main sights of the city where he got to see the enormous plaza called Tiananmen Square, with its huge posters of one of China's former leaders—other schoolchildren about Matthew's age crowded around him, curious to know where he was from.

His blonde hair and gangly height made him stand out a bit in the crowd. The attention was a bit awkward but fun, and he got email addresses from a few would-be pen pals. They also visited the Forbidden City, which, despite its name, was no longer forbidden it was an inviting maze of ancient rooms and halls from which much of imperial China had been ruled.

It was a blur of a day, with so many grand sights and so very many people everywhere you went, rushing along to get to work or to school or to wherever they had to go. Matthew didn't think he'd seen so many people in his entire life as he'd seen in this one day. It was grand, but a little overwhelming. Besides all that, it was a bit hazy in the city, and it was hard to see very far in front of your face. The air felt thick.

After a rest in the room, Matthew got excited all over again, for tonight some Lunar New Year festivities were going to take place. There were lots of traditions associated with the Chinese holiday, such as honoring ancestors and eating dumplings filled with good fortune, but he was most excited about the fireworks and the parade. His mom assured him that it would go right along the street in front of the hotel and that they'd get out early to have a good spot from which to watch the action.

Matthew, indeed, was perched along the sidewalk right up front as the parade began to snake its way down the street. It was noisy and bright and wonderful! There were drummers banging rhythmically on drums, wearing bright costumes of red and gold; there were fireworks going off, here and there, sending bright sparks and showers of multi-colored glitter into the air; there were dancers and acrobats bounding down the street, again in elaborate costumes of bright colors; and, most impressively, there was a great red Chinese dragon (presumably helped along by human puppeteers) winding through the street. He was magnificent, all royal red with golden eyes and real smoke blowing out of its mouth! Unlike the images of European dragons that Matthew was more familiar with, this Chinese dragon was long and lean, like a snake, with four short legs to carry him about. He'd heard these kinds of dragons were also called luck dragons, and it filled his heart with longing. He wouldn't mind some better luck now and again. Sometimes life as a young person could be hard, and it would be nice to be better at sports or to have better grades. Or, turning his strict parents into parents who would let you do anything you wanted. He smiled at that thought not very likely.

Still, he was mesmerized by the dancing snake dragon in its brilliant red, so much so that he found himself slowly approaching it, not really aware of what he was doing, but he just felt he had to touch it, so convinced he was that it must be real. He could faintly hear his mom call his name in the background, but it was too late: Matthew was swept up in the happy chaos of the parade, and he was jostled on all sides by the dancers and performers who were running alongside the dragon. While he was a little bit startled, he was mostly deliriously excited to be caught up in the chaos. After a moment, he found himself quite near the dragon's head—and that's when something truly extraordinary happened. The dragon turned his head to Matthew, looked directly into his eyes, and winked.

At that same moment, Matthew felt a hand on his arm and a good, hard yank as the guide his mom had hired for their trip pulled him out of the parade. He walked him back to his rather stern mom, who, once she was assured that Matthew was okay, was actually pleased to see how happy her sometimes quiet son was.

"Mom, you wouldn't **believe** it," he almost yelled. "The dragon **winked** at me! It did! It winked at **me**." His mom laughed, not wanting to burst his bubble of happiness.

"I'm sure he did, son," she ruffled his hair. "You, my dear, are very special."

After the parade was over, and the last of the fireworks burst gloriously into the air, leaving trails of smoke behind, Matthew and his mom trudged up to bed, tired from all the excitement. Matthew still felt like he wouldn't ever get to sleep, thinking about that amazing dragon, but really, as soon as his head hit the pillow, he was out like a light.

Sometime in the middle of the night, Matthew grunted a bit and rolled over, halfway waking up. As he settled back in to fall back asleep, he heard a soft tapping at the window next to him, followed by a snuffling sound. He lay very still for a moment, sure that he was imagining it, but after a minute, there it was again: tap-tap-tap, snuffle snort, tap-tap-tap, snuffle snort. He listened to this for a while—what felt like a very long time to him—deciding whether he should be afraid or whether he should look. In the end, curiosity got the best of him and he crept quietly out of bed to peek out the window.

It was the dragon! His golden eye was pressed up against the window, peering into study Matthew. Matthew jumped backward, almost falling over the chair behind him, in his surprise. After a second, he looked around to see that his mom was still sleeping, and crept quietly up to the window, pushing it open slightly to see and hear better.

"Hello, lad," the dragon said in a deep and growling voice. "I just had to come see you. It's not often that someone is brave enough to jump into the crowd and stand right next to me." He laughed softly, a low chortle that sounded both amused and impressed. "Why don't you come with me for a while? I'll show you something that tourists almost never get to see."

Matthew hesitated for the briefest of moments, looking back to the sleeping figure of his mom, then grabbed his hoodie and a pair of sneakers and leapt out to the landing.

The long red dragon was floating there, suspended in space—how, Matthew did not know, for it had no wings that he could see—and invited him to jump on his back.

"You, my young friend," he said in his growling voice, "are getting out of the city for a while." With that, he glided off on some mysterious power, soaring higher up into the sky. Matthew could see that, even in the middle of the night, Beijing was filled with lights, from huge buildings and billboards and streets and homes. Eventually, they were just distant twinkles below him as the dragon soared ever higher. It had happened so quickly that Matthew didn't have time to worry or to be afraid. Besides, for some reason, he felt he could trust the dragon; after all, he was a luck dragon.

After a while, the lights started to fade and then there was just blackness below and about them, as they flew outside the city. The dragon was humming a foreign tune and gliding along smoothly, with seemingly no effort at all. Finally, he started to circle what looked like a hilltop and began to descend toward the ground. They landed with a soft thud, and Matthew slipped off the dragon's back.

"Where are we?" he whispered, looking around him at what looked like the densest forest he had ever seen.

"We are in the Hushan Mountains," the dragon replied. "Down below us is part of the Great Wall of China. Wait for a few minutes, and you will start to see." With that, the dragon flew up above him a few feet, and spun three times backwards in a circle; the sun crept slowly upwards from the wrong part of the sky, giving off what felt like late evening light.

Matthew began to see all around him, these mountains so old and worn with time. They were dense with low-growing trees, but he couldn't sense a lot of wildlife in them. They felt alone and empty, but profoundly old and wise.

"Here, lad," the dragon landed next to him again. "Climb back up, and I'll show you around."

The view as the dragon hovered a hundred feet above the mountain was magnificent. Matthew could see what looked like the endless outline of the Great Wall, one of the few things that humans have built that can be seen from outer space, so big was it. But he also noticed something else: the air was so clean and pure that he felt like he was breathing better than he had in days.

The dragon nodded, seemingly reading his thoughts. "Yes, lad, the air here is pure as it isn't in the city." He shook his head. "Too many people, too much pollution. It will surely be the end of us if we aren't careful. That's why I wanted to show you this place, up in the mountains. Surely you understand that these mountains have existed long before humans, and they have seen and known just about everything there is to know. They should be respected and protected."

Matthew nodded in agreement. He could feel how important this place was, and how small he was in it. He was just one small speck amid such a magnificent setting. It was humbling and peaceful at the same time.

"We must get you back. I can't stop time forever, you know," the dragon laughed, and tendrils of smoke curled out of his nostrils. Matthew hopped on for one last magnificent ride, as they glided back into the blackness of night and then, shortly, over the vast lights of the city below them. The dragon glided up to the landing, letting Matthew slide off his back and thump gently down.

"I'll never forget you, luck dragon," Matthew said solemnly. "Or those mountains. Thank you for taking me on such a wonderful journey."

"You are welcome, lad," said the dragon. "And thank you for your bravery. And for caring." With that, the dragon soared upward quickly, as the first faint streaks of dawn started to light the sky. Within a moment, all that was left was a fading puff of smoke.

Matthew crawled back inside, closed the window, and buried himself under the covers. He felt like just about the luckiest person in the world. That's the power of a luck dragon. He drifted off to sleep, dreaming of flying about the greenest mountains in the whole wide world.

Chapter 10:
Butterfly Fairy

Once there was a Butterfly Fairy with wonderful wings. She was driven pixie. Her name was Juana. She was a library overseer of the delightful castle of the Butterfly Fairyland. She adored her activity. She was fond of perusing, so she accepted that her activity is ideal for her. Attractive Prince Turgut was found of perusing as well. He was dazzled by her characteristics.

Butterfly Fairies feared Crystal Fairies, they all accepted that Crystal Fairies are their adversary. One day Queen of Butterfly Fairies welcomed Juana on supper. During supper, Queen talks about Crystal Fairies and she wanted for exchanges with Crystal Fairies. Everything was astonished "How could that be" top dog stated, " Those are troublemakers". In any case, Juana affirmed them the genuine history from the old book, "Years back, Crystal Fairies and Butterfly Fairies were companions, one day a misconception was made between them about gestures of recognition Crystals of Crystal-land and from that time both didn't meet one another" Juana let them know.

Sovereign pick Juana to send Crystal-land for companion transport. Presently, she was all set Crystal-land. Sovereign gave her a sparkling Glass Ball as a guide for voyaging. After voyaging, a night and a day she came to Crystal castle. It was delightfully designed with precious stones and sparkles. Yet, everybody feared Butterfly Fairy, and nobody needed to meet her as they suspected her a troublemaker. Thus, she becomes vexed.

Be that as it may, Merry, King's girl, was a benevolent Crystal Fairy Princess. She became the companion to Juana. She utilized a pixie pony to fly as her wings were harmed. Her amicable conduct made Juana certain. Cheerful welcomed her on supper where she could purchase the message of kinship, from Butterfly Fairy Queen to Crystal-land's King. She came to supper. What's more, gave the message of fellowship to Crystal King. But since of Juana's huge wings, a few bungles have occurred in the royal residence. That drove the King crazy. She got irritated.

Following day, Merry purchased Juana to the most excellent spot of the Crystal-land. It was brimming with shinning precious stones and sparkles. Happy gifted her an excellent Crystal jewelry. In gratitude, Juana gave her shinning Glass Ball. They played there and delighted in a great deal. Joyful enlightened her concerning the yearly Crystal party in the royal residence.

In the night, Juana was all set in the gathering. Joyful made Juana's dress sparkling. She was looking lovely. The gathering was magnificent. It was brimming with happiness.

Nevertheless, a pixie saw Crystal neckband in Juana's neck. She cried "That butterfly pixie is a cheat she has taken Crystal jewelry from Crystal-land" King became angry and requested her to return to Butterfly land, there can be no fellowship."

In stress, she was returning. Out of nowhere, she saw a Witch who was setting off to the Crystal castle. She thought "Perhaps she is going to hurt Crystal Fairies." So, she returned to the royal residence where she saw the witch is obliterating shinning Crystals into dark stones with her dark enchantment. It would be troubled for Crystal Fairies. Juana attempted her best to capture the Witch. Be that as it may, she proved unable. Juana went to Merry. She was aidless.

Juana made her certain to battle with the Witch. At that point without her pixie horse, she flies just because and battled with the Witch. It was difficult turned into the Witch was exceptionally amazing. In any case, Merry and Juana both captured her. In any case, it was past the point of no return as every Crystal was changed into dark stone except for a solitary Crystal. Cheerful and Juana went to that Crystal. They attempted to make it shine as it was previously yet futile. Out of nowhere, they saw the shinning Glass Ball is making the precious stones shinning and beautiful. They put it closer to the Crystal and soon all the Crystal-land got shinning and vivid.

Everybody got glad. Presently, Crystal King was dazzled by Butterfly Fairy Juana. He was appreciative of her fortitude.

What's more, he requested to rebuff the Witch. In any case, Merry didn't permit him to do that. She said "Dear Father, you are committing a similar error as you did years prior. She approached only for a solitary Crystal and we have such a large number of, yet you didn't give her. Try not to rebuff her. We can make her a decent pixie."

At that point she talented her a piece of Crystal jewelry. This agreement completely changed the Witch. She became a companion to the Princess. Everything was glad. Lord acknowledged the companionship from Butterfly Fairies. Juana joyfully came back to Butterfly-land. Presently Butterfly Fairies and Crystal Fairies were companions.

Chapter 11:
Archie's Sister is Kidnapped

A rchie questioned Maggie's loyalty and expressed his irritation with her after he came out of the Wizard's house. The wizard had not given him any proper answers about his siblings or his larger mission. He had left it to Archie to find out all his answers. Archie also could not accept the lies Maggie had told him to bring him here. But Maggie told him that her intentions had been good all along, and she had to follow a protocol. She was not allowed to tell anyone about her mission.

This made Archie realize that sometimes, our friends and family might have to take some questionable steps to make us understand something or to help us out. It does not matter if we like that process or not. The only thing that matters is the outcome. Sometimes we feel like revolting against our parents for certain things they don't let us do, but in time, we will realize they did the right thing.

Archie was not in a position to understand about Paw Island or its rules. Maggie knew that, so she did not say anything. Maggie promised Archie that she would help him find his siblings. She took him to a quaint house in the woods.

That house belonged to Tobby, but Tobby was not a dirty street dog anymore. Tobby told Archie that there was one dog who could help Archie to get to his sister Katty. This dog's name was Doro. Doro was a pug who was Archie's sister, Katty's, best friend. Doro informed Archie and his friends that a circus company had kidnapped Katty.

Archie, Tobby, Maggie, and Doro tried to convince the Paw Island Council to allow them to undertake a rescue mission. But the Council would not allow it. However, they visited the Wizard and asked for his advice. Wizard Coco told them to follow their hearts, to be there for each other, and, above all, to put family above all rules and protocols.

True friendship can be tested at a time of crisis. Archie's friends could let him go alone, but they helped him. A friend should always support another friend in need.

Archie's test was complete. And now his real journey was about to begin. Coco did not give any hint about what it would be. He just suggested that he find Maggie. Maggie would guide him accordingly. Archie had a lot of questions to ask. But he felt that Coco was not in the mood to answer any questions. Coco was about to leave when Archie asked, "You said my siblings are here - what they are doing here? Who brought them here? And what if I do not feel the urge to go on the given mission or stay here? Are my parents alive?"

Coco stopped on his way out and turned to answer. He said, "Archie, patience is the key to success. You will get all the answers when the time is right. But you need to be prepared first. This test proved that you are worthy of being trained. But you need to be worthy to receive these answers. Now you know the source. It is your job to find out the rest. I am not going to serve you everything you need on a silver platter. We believe in determination, discipline, and persistence. Do not rush."

Coco stormed out of the room, and Archie stood there silently. His head was spinning. He was confused and a bit frustrated. He hated twisted and riddle-like answers. There was no point in standing in that room anymore, so he also stormed out of the house. He saw Maggie was waiting outside eagerly, as though she had already known Archie was going to need her.

This strange land and its strange dogs, Archie thought.

"What are you doing here?" asked Archie. Maggie was waiting for Archie; she was curious to know how the test had gone. But Archie's expression showed his inner irritation about the whole situation. So, she decided to remain silent. Archie repeated his question more insistently.

Maggie suppressed her curiosity. She replied casually, "I am actually waiting for you. I know that the wizard must have told you to come to me for further guidance to tour the island. You still do not know about this island and its roads. So, I thought I could wait here for you. So how was your experience? Have you discovered anything interesting? You can share with me, you know!"

Archie realized there was no point in being mad at Maggie because she'd had nothing to do with the entire test or Coco's reluctance to reply to his questions. After all, this whole trial was about anger, hatred, and these types of emotions - *and* how he should fight them. So, he took some deep breaths and replied, "I finally realized the futility of being angry with someone for so long, and the disadvantages of hatred. I also realized that humans are not all bad or our enemies. To survive, we should always help each other and cooperate with each other. There is a hidden bliss in the ability to help others. I had a lot of questions, though, and the wizard refused to answer any of them. He said I must get my answers through persistence and patience. And I have no idea what to do next. So, tell me, are you going to help me in my pursuit?"

Maggie knew that the wizard loved riddles. And unfortunately, she had no idea how to help her friend. But she also realized her friend needed motivation and emotional support. He was already feeling lost. So, she said carefully, "I do not know how to help you, but if you decide to do something, I will always be there for you because that's what a friend should do. But you have to decide - what is the first thing you need to do? According to the law here, now is the time you should be visiting the training center and meeting the instructors. But if you feel that there is something more important than that, then do it; otherwise, you will always feel restless inside yourself."

Archie smiled and replied, "I know that you want to support me, and you consider me a friend. I also care about you, but I need to know something from you. Did you know that my entire experience was crafted by a Wizard or by a prophecy of this island? You had asked me to trust you, but you never told me that I am nothing but one of your missions. So, tell me, how can I can trust you!? What if I don't feel like fulfilling some stupid prophecy of this land? I don't even know whether my siblings are here or not. You played me once - now tell me, Maggie, how I can consider you as a friend and guardian angel after all your lies."

Archie had every right to be mad about the whole situation. And now was not a good time to make him appreciate the implications and reasoning behind the situation. Maggie replied calmly, "You will get all your answers soon; then, you will understand why I couldn't tell you about my secret mission. The wizard can never lie, so if he said that your siblings are here, then it is true. And no one can give you all the solutions, as the wizard said. I know you have no reason to trust me again, but you have to realize one thing - whatever we have done, everything was related only to your safety. I cannot tell you where your siblings are right now because I do not know.

But I can take you to someone who can help you to figure out all these answers, or at least tell you about your siblings. Come with me."

The calmness of Maggie's voice somehow pacified Archie's resentment. Sometimes our friends and family have to take steps to protect us or to teach us something, and it is not necessary that we will always like their methods. But before we start judging them, we should always try to understand the intention behind their actions. Then, Archie remembered a story Paul had told him.

It had been Paul's birthday. In the morning, when his mother was busy baking a cake for him, he took her favorite paintings and used them in making a house for Coco. His mother was very sad after discovering what he had done with the painting, but she did not rebuke him or say anything. However, she took some of his favorite toy cars and hid those for a few days. He was angry and frustrated when he failed to find his toys. But after two days, he realized how his mother had felt when he spoiled her paintings. Though he didn't like the method, his mother had to make him understand the lesson. But, Paul thought, it was better than scolding or ill-treatment. Carol's intentions were good.

Coco's methods of making Archie understand the problems with feelings like hatred and anger were also questionable. But his attempt had, indeed, been successful. Archie would never forget the teaching.

So, Archie did not argue with Maggie anymore. He simply nodded in agreement. Maggie took him to a small house in the woods and knocked on the door. It was Tobby who opened the door.

The Tobby Archie had known a dirty and street dog. But this Tobby was a healthy, clean, and well-maintained dog. Archie quickly recognized him from his doe-shaped eyes. His eyes expressed how eagerly he had been waiting for Archie.

Archie and Maggie entered Tobby's modest hut. It was a quaint little house. The Tobby Archie had known was messy and rude. He had seemed like a rogue street dog, but his present-day living conveyed a whole new story. Tobby knew Archie had a lot to ask him. Tobby served them both hot bone broth and said, "Archie, first of all, I am happy to see that you finally reached Paw Island. I had a mission to bring you here. But those two boys chased you and hurt you. It was unexpected. That was not included in our plan. But when I came to know that Maggie had discovered you, I felt relieved. I know I have deceived you. But that was not the right time to make you understand what was happening. You are very important to everyone here. We have been waiting for you for so long."

Tobby had already anticipated the questions and Archie's thoughts about everything. His honest confession brought a broad smile to Archie's face. He replied, "I have no complaints. I may not understand your ways, but I know that you tried to protect me. You people are weird - but in a good way! However, I want to meet my siblings and especially my little sister Katty. You know how much I wanted to meet her. Maggie told me that you could help me in locating them."

Tobby smiled and said, "Your sister has been living with us for quite some time, and she is already on her first mission! Let me call Doro - he knows her exact location. But you are not trained yet. So, I do not know whether the authorities will allow you to go outside Paw Island or not. But I will try my best to help you, my friend."

Tobby called his aides and asked him to bring in Doro. After a while, Doro came in. Doro was a tiny puppy with a small tail. He had the face of someone who is always happy. Tobby introduced Doro to Archie. But Archie was not expecting the greeting Doro gave him.

Doro jumped up to hug Archie and hugged him so hard he was about to suffocate him. Archie had no idea what was happening. Then Doro started crying. Tobby and Maggie were also confused. Doro said, "Katty is my best friend, and she is always talking about you. I am just coming from the council office. I went there to get an update on Katty's mission. It is her first mission, so I was very worried. But then I got the unexpected news. I have no heart to tell it to you, Archie."

Archie, Tobby, and Maggie did not say anything, and Doro continued sobbing. Archie's heart was racing, and he was imagining all the worst scenarios he could imagine. Doro continued, "Katty was carrying out a mission of rescuing a litter of abandoned newborns. But some people from Coast Circus kidnapped her. The council is sending a team to rescue her, but I do not know exactly what is happening to her. I am so sorry, Archie! I know how long you have been waiting to see your sister."

Maggie and Tobby fell silent after this unexpected twist of events. They had been expecting a happy reunion, but they now did not know how to react. Archie snarled, "See, Maggie, why I do not believe in your stupid missions? My sister has been kidnapped because of the strange way of life of this fantasy land."

Tobby tried to mollify him and said, "It is because of this land that you are getting another chance to see your sister. These missions and training empower us and unify us. We are not just meant to be the pets of humans. We play a great role in society. We help military soldiers in their livelihood, we help blind people to walk, we keep lonely people company, and we help as guard dogs. Again, as you can see, we are an important part of society. You are new here, and I do not expect you to understand everything instantly. I know you are upset after getting this news. But *your* sister is *our* sister. We will do everything we can to free her from the circus company."

Archie was upset, but his brain was working. He realized they would need as much help as possible to rescue his sister. He could never just rely on the council and their typical rescue missions. It was his family, and he had to go. So, he remained silent and did not argue with Tobby. Archie, Maggie, Tobby, and Doro rushed towards the Council office. Tobby said to the officer, "Hi, we have received the news of Katty's kidnap. This is Archie, Katty's brother. He came here today, and the Wizard has already tested his worthiness. Four of us want to come with the search party to rescue Katty."

Archie had no plans for a group search; however, he felt the keenness in Tobby's voice. That convinced him to stay silent. He could trust them. This was the first time Archie had felt like he had real friends. They were even willing to risk their lives and well-being for the well-being of Archie's sister. Archie was not alone anymore. He had good friends who would always be with him. Good friends always help a friend in need. They support in bad times and keep us motivated. They encourage us to be better and do well.

The officer replied, "Tobby, I understand. Every brother wants to take care of his sister. And Katty's other siblings are not here; for now, they are involved in other missions. But I cannot allow

Archie to go on this rescue mission without any proper training. This is against protocol."

Archie finally said, "Ma'am, I understand the whole "protocol thing." But I am not officially part of the Paw Island way of life. So, no protocol can stop me from protecting my sister. I respect your rules, but you cannot tell me what to do. I am going."

Tobby, Doro, and Maggie knew they were bound to follow the rules of Paw Island. But they could not leave Archie alone. Tobby said, "Archie, we must go to the wizard. He is wise and old. He can give us good advice."

Archie and his friends revisited Coco's house. Coco had already got the news of Katty's kidnap, and he was expecting Archie. Doro asked, "Wizard, we know it is wrong to disobey the council. But we want to help Archie. What should we do?"

The wizard replied, "Disobeying rules is wrong. But not helping a friend in need is unethical. We should always prioritize our family. Katty is alone and probably scared. You should help Archie to get her back. Take this cloak with you. It will help you to be invisible. And these potions will give you strength as per your capabilities. You will need these. My blessing is with you. And Archie, son, you do not need the training to help Katty. Because it is not a mission - it is a real-life crisis. Always stay calm. God bless you."

Just after sunset, Archie, Tobby, Maggie, and Doro began a new journey - the journey to rescue Katty.

Chapter 12:
Dagi the Happy Shark

Far out in the heart of the big blue sea, there lived a shark whose name was Dagi. Dagi was a beautiful blue shark, with a wide, big-toothed smile. He was also an excellent swimmer.

When Dagi was a baby shark, he loved swimming around the sea and exploring what lay in the water near their home. Every day, Dagi would wake up, and after having breakfast, he would wave goodbye to his mother with his little fins and dart outside their underwater cave to look for a new adventure.

Outside, he would be joined by his friends, Pago and Tina. They would first go around the neighborhood to see what's new, and then they would extend their forays into the nearby forest of seaweed and coral reefs. Every so often, a family would have new kids, and it was always fun to meet them and welcome them to the neighborhood. Pago was a little older, and Tina was a little younger than Dagi, but that was never a problem for them, and they always found many things that they liked in common. Sometimes, they would notice a new growth on a coral or a missing branch in the seaweed, and they would play guessing games on what might have happened to it.

"Maybe a sea cow ate it," Dagi would say.

"Or maybe someone made a nest with it," Tina would say.

"Or, or, or, maybe Miss Simone, the octopus, took it to sweep the floor with," Pago would say excitedly, then they would move to the next area to see what's new.

Sometimes, they would notice a pufferfish nest and go to marvel at it and try to count the circles and ridges.

"One, two, three, four, five," counted Tina.

"Six, seven, eight, nine," continued Dagi.

"Ten!!" They all said in unison. "But what comes after ten?" Did they wonder? "Oh well, we'll be going to school soon, and we will learn everything there."

And so, it came to be. They started school in the next season, and everything was lovely. They liked their new schoolmates and made friends with most of them. There was a lot to learn, and the teachers were accommodating and kind, and Miss Tocci was even funny!

However, there was this one classmate named Rah. He did not seem to like the others very much, and he kept mostly to himself even during recess. Whenever anyone came close, he would swim away, and he hardly ever spoke in class. One day, Dagi approached him and said, in a friendly manner, "Hello

Rah, how are you today?" but Rah did not answer him. He just turned away and continued to sulk.

When Dagi got home, and they were talking about how the day was, Dagi asked his parents why some people are sulky, and he related to them his short encounter with Rah earlier in the day.

"Maybe he is having a problem adjusting to the new school," said his mom.

"Or maybe he has a speech problem." said his dad. "You know, some people stutter or stammer, but it goes away with time and with practice," he added.

Dagi always marveled at how wise and insightful his parents were. "And what can I do to help him?" he asked.

"Just keep being his friend," answered his dad.

"And maybe try teaching him a new song, like the one we taught you when you were learning to swim and would sometimes be afraid. Do you remember it?" asked his mom.

"Oh, yes! I had forgotten about that song. Let's sing it, mama; remind me the words please," Dagi pleaded.

"Oh, alright," said his mom. But first, go get ready for bed, then I'll be with you shortly to sing the song.

"Yay!" said Dagi, and off he went to get ready for bed.

When his mom came in, Dagi was ready to start right away. "Okay, do you remember how we start?" Mom asked.

"Yes," replied Dagi.

"Breathe in, and hold,

One, two, three, then breathe out

"Good job!" said mom.

"Breathe in, and hold,

Four, five, six, whistle out," sang mom

"Yes, yes, I remember now!" cried Dagi. Then in unison, they sang.

Breathe in, and hold,

Seven, eight, nine, flap your fins

Breathe in, and hold,

Up to ten, let's return."

"Now, I remember it all," said Dagi, "Can we sing it one more time?"

"Alright, dear; just this once, then it's bedtime," said his mom.

"Breathe in, and hold,

One, two, three, then breathe out

Breathe in, and hold,

Four, five, six, whistle out

Breathe in, and hold,

Seven, eight, nine, flap your fins

Breathe in, and hold,

Up to ten, let's return."

"You two sound terrific." said dad. "But it's bedtime now, so goodnight, son," he said as he kissed Dagi goodnight. Dad and mom both went out. Dagi was glad to have remembered the breathing song and couldn't wait to teach it to Rah. He thought about the song lyrics again as he drifted off to sleep.

The next day was the beginning of a long weekend. As usual, Tina and Pago came around, and the trio went seeking adventure. They swam much further than they were used to, and Pago noticed that Dagi was quiet most of the way.

"Hey, Dagi, what's up, buddy? You are very quiet today."

"Oh, nothing," said Dagi as he swept a pebble aside with his fin, and they continued in silence. Tina, Dagi, and Pago did not realize how far they were from home until they tried to ascend and found that they were already deep inside a cavern. "What do we do now?" asked Tina with fear in her voice.

"Oh, my! I was so deep in thought about Rah that I did not even realize where we are!" shouted Dagi, who had just now snapped from his reverie.

"What about Rah? And what d-d-d-do we do now?" Asked Pago

"Oh, you know, how he's always quiet at school, in class, and at recess."

Just then, they heard a loud splashing from the darker part of the cave, moving swiftly toward them. The three turned and swam as fast as their little fins could carry them, but they were not fast enough. They heard growling and turned back to see what it was. A great white shark with pointy, gleaming teeth was coming toward them.

"What itty bitty little dudes! Go get them, bro!" He growled.

From the little light streaming into the cave, the youngsters saw a familiar figure swimming toward them. When he got closer, they saw it was Rah! He swam hesitatingly toward them but growled just like his brother. Taking advantage of his slower pace, they turned and fled out of the cave. They heard a loud, angry growl behind them, but they did not turn back, and neither did he come after them. For the rest of the weekend, the three friends played close to home and were a little apprehensive about going back to school when it restarted.

Come the next school day, Dagi, Tina, and Pago swam to school together and kept close together all day, making sure to steer clear of Rah. They did the same on the following day. The school was no longer fun for them. They were always afraid that Rah would do something to scare them even more. Dagi was very unhappy with the situation, and he said to his friends, "Tina, Pago, let us try to do something about this. Maybe we can ask Rah why he behaved that way in the cave."

"Ummm, well, alright," they agreed half-heartedly.

At recess, they slowly swam toward where Rah was, and this time, he did not swim away or growl at them.

"Hello, Rah," They said timidly, but he did not answer.

"That day at the cave, you were very mean to us. Why?" asked Dagi.

Rah was silent for a while, then he told them that his big brother, Basa, was the bully in their neighborhood, and he wanted Rah to be just like him. He added that Basa had told him to have no other friend but him.

"Oh, how sad, said Dagi. "Here, I will teach you a song that my mom taught me; it helps me not to be afraid. Okay?"

"'Okay!" said Tina, who always liked songs. Dagi remembered then that he had not yet taught it to his friends.

"Pago, Rah, wanna learn it, too?

"Sure," said Pago.

"Okay," said Rah.

Okay. It is called the breathing song. Breathe in, hold, and breath out. Now sing after me."

"Breathe in, and hold,

One, two, three, then breathe out

Breathe in, and hold,

Four, five, six, whistle out

Breathe in, and hold,

Seven, eight, nine, flap your fins

Breathe in, and hold,

Up to ten, let's return."

Oh, it is such a good song! said Tina. "It makes me feel relaxed," added Pago.

"How about you, Rah?" asked Dagi.

It's alright, I guess," said Rah.

Okay, let's sing it again.

"Breathe in, and hold,

One, two, three, then breathe out

Breathe in, and hold,

Four, five, six, whistle out

Breathe in, and hold,

Seven, eight, nine, flap your fins

Breathe in, and hold,

Up to ten, let's return."

"I actually do feel much better," said Rah.

The three friends looked at each other happily.

"Told you, it works!" Said Dagi.

"Okay, fins in. Friends on three! One, two, three!"

"Friends!" they all shouted happily and went back to class, giggling.

After that, every day at recess, Rah joined them, and they always started and ended the recess with the breathing song. Sometimes, when Rah couldn't' sleep at night, too, he sang it to himself. One day, his brother, Basa, heard him and gruffly asked him, "What are you singing? Why are you singing?

"My friend at school taught me a breathing song. I sing it to relax and not to feel afraid," Rah replied. He was no longer afraid to stand up to his brother. Basa noticed this and was also perplexed that his little brother had friends at school. The tune for the breathing song, however, was so catchy, Basa asked Rah to teach it to him.

"Breathe in, and hold,

One, two, three, then breathe out

Breathe in, and hold,

Four, five, six, whistle out

Breathe in, and hold,

Seven, eight, nine, flap your fins

Breathe in, and hold,

Up to ten, let's return."

At the very same time, Dagi was singing the same song with his parents at bedtime. He was no longer afraid or anxious, but he was glad that the song had brought joy to his friends, and especially Rah.

"Breathe in, and hold,

One, two, three, then breathe out

Breathe in, and hold,

Four, five, six, whistle out

Breathe in, and hold,

Seven, eight, nine, flap your fins

Breathe in, and hold,

Up to ten, let's return."

Conclusion

As you continue to help yourself fall asleep every night, I encourage you to make sure that you always maintain the best sleep routine possible. Preparing your children for bed and winding down the same way every single night is a great way to let your body know it is time to sleep. Do you know why that is? The answer is: routine!

Moment by Moment, Ever-Changing

Mindfulness takes practice. You may need to work on it as you would any other skill.

A soccer player practices footwork. A dancer trains muscles. A mathematician solves problems step by step. You cannot master your mind without practicing MINDFUL ME skills every day.

Meditation is staying alert and resting your mind in its calm, relaxed, and natural state.

So, remember, mindfulness is a choice. Your choice. Being a MINDFUL ME is about connecting the dots between feeling an emotion, thinking a thought, and acting on them. It is about using meditation to train your mind and expand your heart.

Without mindfulness, you might react quickly to your thoughts and feelings, and do something you'll wish you hadn't. With mindfulness, you can find your way to your WISDOM MIND, which is open, accepting, and generous. Everything in the world changes from one minute to another. That's true for your thoughts and feelings too. If you were distracted a minute ago, remember that minute is over. You have another chance to be mindful in this present moment. With each new breath, you can pay attention.

Your body and mind love having the same hints that it is time to do something like eat or go to sleep. When you take the time to make your sleep routine a habit, your body and mind begin to learn that this routine means it is time to go to sleep. Soon, your body will automatically begin winding down and getting tired when you start the routine, even long before you actually finish it! This is the magic of your body and mind.

As you continue to repeat the habit and see these benefits, you will find yourself having a much better sleep every single night. Plus, it will become much easier for you to fall asleep because you are actually tired and ready for a good rest. This means that when waking up, you will be ready to enjoy plenty of great fun with your friends and family all over again!

Remember: a good night's sleep is an important part of waking up feeling refreshed and ready to have a great day.

You should always practice doing everything you can to help have a wonderful night's sleep every single night.

Through mindfulness meditation, an individual will become aware of what is happening within as well as become more adept at allowing distractions and frustrations to flow leaving the person more peacefully.

Thank you, and I wish you many wonderful dreams. Goodnight!